GUARANTEED MONIES

Getting the Most Out
of Your Hard-Earned
Social Security Money

Roy Snarr

Table of Contents

What Others Say About Roy Snarr

Social Security and a sense of humor — this combination does not come about very often. Roy Snarr's guide to Social Security combines humor with a frank discussion on Social Security. The Social Security Act was signed into law on August 14, 1935, and today provides benefits to 64 million folks nationwide. In 2019, a little over $1 trillion was paid to Social Security recipients. Social Security is a very large government program, and many people believe that Social Security is also very complicated. However, Mr. Snarr breaks down the Social Security rules in easy-to-understand terms and combines a unique sense of humor to keep the reader engaged and asking for more.

Whether you are single, married, divorced, a surviving spouse, or a public employee, this Social Security guide will help you understand your Social Security claiming strategies, resulting in larger benefits over your lifetime and that of a surviving spouse (if applicable).

Mr. Snarr has earned the National Social Security Advisor certificate, which denotes advanced education in Social Security and related claiming strategies. Earning the National Social Security Advisor certificate, Mr. Snarr has taken an in-depth class on Social Security and passed an assessment. He has joined a limited number of advisors that have earned this certificate nationwide.

I commend you for reading this guide on Social Security. Mr. Snarr will help you understand your benefits and the options that are available.

Marc Kiner, CPA
National Social Security Advisor certificate holder
Creator of the National Social Security Advisor certificate program

---

Roy's ability to take a complex topic and turn it into tangible and understandable terms sets Roy's book apart from the many books on the complex rules of Social Security. Roy's story about his mom became the catalyst for his passion for helping consumers create an empowered retirement. His practical guidance and "Fun Facts" on navigating the important Social Security claiming decision make this book a must read before reaching for the Social Security "on" button. If you are wondering what you need to consider before filing for benefits or if you simply need an overall guide on how Social Security works, this book is for you!

Heather Schreiber, RICP®
HLS Retirement Consulting

Introduction

My Goal in Writing

The goal of writing this short book is to help you become more familiar with how your Social Security benefits are calculated. By having a good understanding of the Social Security Administration's (SSA) formulas, you will be better positioned for retirement and, most importantly, more confident. The information in this book will guide you in making a more informed claiming decision that considers the variables that are unique to you.

One of the many reasons it is important to pick the best filing strategy is because your decision is generally a permanent one, with one exception. You have the option to withdraw your application once in a lifetime — but only within the first 12 months of filing.

If you take that option, you must pay back all the benefits you received, but it provides you with a complete do-over to file at a later date. Interest-free loan, you say? Not really. It's your money to begin with, and there can be unique situations where this option might be a good idea (but usually it is not).

After that, you will be living with your Social Security check based on your filing age, and you will not be able to change it. There is an option to stop your benefit after 12 months once you hit your full retirement age, but this will also stop all other benefits from being paid off of your record, such as a spousal benefit.

Chapter 1

Social Security Planning

It truly amazes me how little Social Security is talked about in financial planning strategies. Almost every client I currently work with and have worked with receives little to no guidance regarding considerations when making their Social Security filing decision.

Why? Well, there are a few reasons: Social Security planning typically does not create revenue. Some advisors *do* have the ability to charge a fee for a consultation that can include a discussion around Social Security, but most do not.

Another reason (which I believe to be the main reason) is that most agents and advisors don't have enough knowledge to confidently recommend ideas or strategies. It takes a lot of time, effort, energy, and dedication to learn the Social Security system and stay up to date with changes. As my business grew, I started noticing this huge deficit in the retirement planning community; one of the most important decisions that directly affects retirement income was being overlooked.

This is why I was determined to learn how Social Security actually works and how it can benefit my clients in their retirement planning. Today, I host regular educational workshops at a variety of community colleges and universities throughout central Texas. The classes are free for the community to attend.

During these classes, I go over high-level filing strategies to help folks just like you make retirement planning as easy as possible. I also send out regular video vlogs about the most common questions I get asked about Social Security. You are free to sign up for my newsletter at RoySnarr.com. It's educational only; I won't try and sell you a timeshare. This book is much more detailed than most of my classes and radio shows, mainly because there's not enough time to go over everything during those platforms. Can you imagine sitting in on a Social Security class for eight hours straight? I didn't think so.

My Commitment to You

I will do my best to break down in simple terms and examples how Social Security works and some strategies that may help you make a more informed filing decision. Most likely, you will learn a lot. Some will be old news, but most should be very interesting and useful. Everybody's situation is different, so some of the content may not apply to you the same way it applies to others.

There may be information that is not covered about Social Security, simply because it is too complex to cover in a high-level overview. I am not going to bore you with the lengthy history of Social Security and the various changes that have occurred over the last 75 years. Rather, I am going to focus on relevant content that affects the majority of folks.

The Reason I Do What I Do

When I was about 14 years old, my mother became permanently disabled. She was sideswiped by a driver who ran a stop sign. The accident created an onset of continuing problems. Over the next few years, my mother was diagnosed with degenerative disc disease. She lost her job, we lost our house, and most of her savings and retirement was decimated in the dot-com bubble. The only source of income we had was her Social Security Disability Insurance income (SSDI) check. Of course, I had no idea what Social Security was at the time, but it truly was a lifesaver.

The older I became, the more intrigued I was about finance and how money works. It blew my mind that one single life event could cause such financial distress for us. Fueling my curiosity and passion for helping people, I started working with a large financial firm while studying cultural anthropology in college. Fast-forward to today; my mother has worked with me side by side for over 10 years. We run the family company, Snarr Financial & Insurance Services, Inc. We are so fortunate to have the ability to help thousands of people coast to coast learn about protecting their finances and maximizing their Social Security benefits.

Thank you for taking the time out of your day, night, and life to read this book.

Now, let's get to it!

Chapter 2

The Importance of Social Security

The Social Security system can be a maze to navigate. Filing your Social Security benefits is one of the most important financial decisions (if not the most important) for a successful retirement. Why? Well, Social Security provides a guaranteed stream of lifetime income that most Americans count on. You work your entire life, pay taxes, and then when you go to retire, you receive another paycheck you can rely upon.

Social Security in its purest form is quite simple; you work, pay taxes, retire (or simply get older), and then you get "paid back" for all your years of contributing. Basically, it's money out of one pocket (yours) to another pocket (the SSA) and back to your pocket again. This back and forth takes an average of 40 plus years of work for most people. In the meantime, you are not eligible to access the money unless you are disabled or widowed (more on that later).

When you become eligible — not on your terms but the terms dictated by the SSA — you can start slowly getting your money back. Once you are ready and meet the eligibility requirements, your payable benefit is calculated based on a series of set formulas by the SSA. This is where knowing how your benefit is calculated based on particular circumstances (age, marital status, employment, et cetera) is crucial.

Far too often, people file for their benefits without consulting a professional, simply because they think it is a good idea or because they "can." Now, there's nothing wrong with taking your benefit when you want to take it; after all, it's your money! However, if most people knew the ins and outs and the pros and cons of the various filing strategies, we would be talking about different statistics.

Many folks start collecting their benefits at age 62, the earliest eligibility (unless you are disabled or widowed). Again, there's nothing wrong with taking your benefits early, and sometimes it can make a lot more sense to do so. The whole concept of Social Security is to provide income to help supplement retirement expenses.

After all, Social Security was created in 1935 to provide the aging and retiring population some guaranteed income in the hopes that they would live above the poverty line. For most people of this era, a Social Security check was all they had to look forward to in retirement income.

Today, Social Security makes up roughly 40% of retirement income for baby boomers. The other 60% comes from pensions (if you still have one), personal savings, and individual retirement accounts (401(k)s, IRAs). Most Americans will be relying upon 60% of what they have saved to make it through retirement or golden years. These golden years can turn to "rusted years" quickly if the risks are not understood and mitigated.

There are a lot of risks in retirement. Perhaps the most prevalent risk is longevity. Could you outlive your savings? And if you do, will your Social Security check be enough? Most people will spend 20-30 years in retirement, something that never happened during the 1940s. Most people worked until they died, which was not hard to do when the life expectancy was around 60 years of age. Today it is much higher, and you can expect to live into your 80s, statistically speaking. Keep in mind if you take your Social Security benefit early, it will be permanently reduced, affecting many years of cash flow. More on this coming right up. But first, let's take a quick look at how you become eligible for benefits in the first place.

Chapter 3

Social Security Credits

Social Security credits are determined by your earnings record. In 2020, you must make at least $1,410 in the year to earn one credit. You can earn up to four credits per year by making at least $5,640 in the calendar year. Each year, the SSA typically adjusts the minimum quarterly earning requirements to adjust for the cost of living and wage increases. You need 40 credits to become eligible for Social Security benefits (generally around 10 years of work). These credits can be earned throughout your working life; they do not need to be earned consecutively.

Disability eligibility is different. Later in the book, I go over the charts and the credits needed. When it comes to filing for SSDI, you may want to seek out an attorney who specializes in Social Security disability. Why? There are lots of rules and restrictions to claiming this benefit; hence the reason entire law firms are dedicated to Social Security disability.

So, you have more than 10 years of working history? Congrats, you are part of an exclusive club of almost everybody, but it's a great club to be a part of because it will help you! The more you work and the higher your pay, the greater your Social Security benefit will be, to an extent.

What the SSA does is look at your highest 35 years of earnings, indexed for inflation up to age 60. Then they divide your total indexed earnings by 420 (which equals the number of months in 35 years) to calculate your AIME, or average indexed monthly earnings. (Earnings after age 60 are used in the calculation but not indexed for inflation.) Your AIME is then put through a bend point formula to determine your primary insurance amount (PIA), which your full retirement age (FRA) benefit amount (e.g., your monthly check).

You are entitled to 100% of your benefit at your FRA. Your benefits are calculated from the PIA; you will either see a reduction on your PIA or an increase from your PIA amount, depending on your filing age.

The reasoning behind the bend point formula is to replace a higher percentage of a lower income earner's earnings. Benefits are limited based on the Federal Insurance Contributions Act (FICA) wage cap (for 2020, that number is $137,700). For instance, if you are at your FRA in 2020 and have maximum earnings, you will receive roughly $3,011 per month. In some rare cases, if an individual had earned a significant income (maximum table earnings for Social Security) since the age of 22 and delayed taking their Social Security benefit until they reached age 70 in 2020, they could earn as much as $3,790 per month. However, the average Social Security benefit paid today is roughly $1,428 per month.

PIA formula to determine your FRA benefit amount:

- For a person who first becomes eligible for benefits in 2020 (or who dies in 2020 before becoming eligible for benefits), their PIA will be the sum of:

Bend Points below

a. 90% of the first $960 of their AIME, plus

b. 32% of their AIME over $960 up to $5,785, plus

c. 15% of their average indexed monthly earnings over $5,785

Having fun with math yet? Luckily, SSA calculates this for you, but in case you were curious (or had nothing to do on a Saturday), you can now calculate your PIA.

Fun Facts

Thankfully, there is an inflation-adjusted aspect to your earnings records. "High pay" of $100 in 1960 is a lot different than today. The inflation adjustment only applies up to age 60. After that, the SSA will not adjust any future earnings for inflation.

At age 62, your bend points and indexing factors are set, meaning your FRA benefit is set at 62, but it can go up if you earn a higher income from age 62 and beyond.

You can check your earnings history by logging into your SSA account online. If you haven't done so yet, you should. If there are any discrepancies that you find, you can take steps to correct them. (Can you imagine a massive government entity ever making a mistake? Well, they sure do, and it happens all the time.)

Social Security rounds down (lowering your payment) to the nearest dollar — which is significant when you consider that as of October 2019, roughly 64,000,000 people are receiving benefits, and that number is rapidly growing!

Summary:

You work, pay taxes, retire, and are paid back a portion of what you contributed to Social Security taxes. The generation behind you works, pays taxes, and helps fund the system. Like everything else that involves money, formulas are applied to calculate what you are entitled to (FRA, PIA, AIME, bend points, et cetera.) You don't have to know all of the intricacies, but it is good to understand at a high level how your benefit is calculated so that you can make an informed decision on WHEN you want to take your benefit.

Chapter 4

Cost of Living Adjustments

One of the many great features of Social Security is the ability for your benefit to increase year after year while you are receiving your payments. Cost of living (COLA) adjustments are not guaranteed to happen every year. There have been three years with big fat zeros in 2010, 2011, and 2016. The reason for the COLA is to ensure that the purchasing power of your Social Security benefits is not eroded by inflation.

The COLA adjustments are based on the percentage increase in the Consumer Price Index for Urban Wage Earners and Clerical Workers (CPI-W) — from the third quarter of the last year a COLA was determined to the third quarter of the current year. If there is no increase, there can be no COLA. The CPI-W is determined by the Bureau of Labor Statistics at the Department of Labor. It is the official measure used by the SSA to calculate COLAs.

Cost of living adjustments affect every type of Social Security benefit, with the increase taking place the following year on your January check (technically, the check is cut in December, but you receive it in January). COLAs are great but are not always accurate predictors of actual inflation or cost of living increases, particularly for retirees whose spending habits differ from urban workers.

The other very important aspect to look at is Medicare Part B premiums, which can increase every year, reducing your overall Social Security benefit net cash flow. (For instance, if you are receiving $2,000 per month gross and paying $144.60 (2020) for Part B, your Social Security check is now $1,855.40. If there is a COLA of 2% it will be added to your $2,000 bringing it up to $2,040 but if Part B premiums are $144.60 now your Social Security payment is $2,040–$144.60 = $1,895.40.)

So yes, you did receive an increase, but it was not a full 2% realization since Part B went up. There are rules in place that help protect most folks against Part B increases so their Social Security benefit will not decrease from the prior year. This is called the hold harmless agreement and is just another fun way our government plays with the numbers.

Chapter 5

Full Retirement Age

When you reach your FRA, you are eligible for 100% of your PIA. Many people assume that their FRA is 65. Perhaps their parents informed them that 65 was their FRA, or they thought that since people are generally eligible for Medicare at age 65, Social Security FRA was the same. Your true FRA is based on your year of birth. See the chart below that nicely illustrates your FRA:

Birth Year	Full Retirement
1943-1954	66
1955	66 and 2 months
1956	66 and 4 months
1957	66 and 6 months
1958	66 and 8 months
1959	66 and 10 months
1960 and later	67

67 is the **new 65** for Baby Boomers

You are generally eligible for your benefit when you are 62 and 1 month. The SSA wants you to be age 62 for the entire month before you can start receiving your benefits. Your benefit will be reduced if you take it before your FRA. One reduction is based on age; the other is possible if you are still working while collecting your benefit before your FRA. If you wait until age 70, you will receive your maximum benefit amount. However, your benefit does not increase past age 70, other than for a potential cost of living adjustment, so never wait beyond age 70 to file. Basically, the closer to God you are, the more the SSA will pay you since there will be fewer monthly payments over the span of your life. The following is an example of how this works:

Let's assume your FRA is 67, and your FRA benefit equals $2,000 per month (PIA). If you want to take your benefit at age 62, you will be paid — wait for it — 30% less, which equals $600, so your new monthly benefit is $1,400. If your FRA is 66, the reduction is less. It's only a 25% reduction if you file at 62 and is based on how many months before your FRA you file. For example, if you filed at age 64, the SSA would base your reduction on the number of months prior to FRA you are at that point.

However, if you delay claiming your benefit beyond your FRA, it will grow at 8% for each 12-month delay. It will not grow 8% per year starting at age 62. The 8% annual increases begin after you have already reached your full retirement age.

For example:

- Let's assume your FRA is 66, and you wait until age 70 to file for your benefit. You'll have four years of earning 8% on your PIA (32% more) as follows:

- PIA = $2,000 X .32 = $640. Now your benefit amount is $2,640 per month.

- A person whose FRA is age 67 will receive a maximum of 24% more since there is one less year to earn 8%.

- Age 67 to 70 is three years, thus.08 X 3 =.24

You don't have to wait a full 12 months either; the delayed retirement credits you earn are calculated monthly at the rate of two-thirds of 1% per month. So, for every month of waiting, you get paid a tad more. Let's visualize this for simplicity:

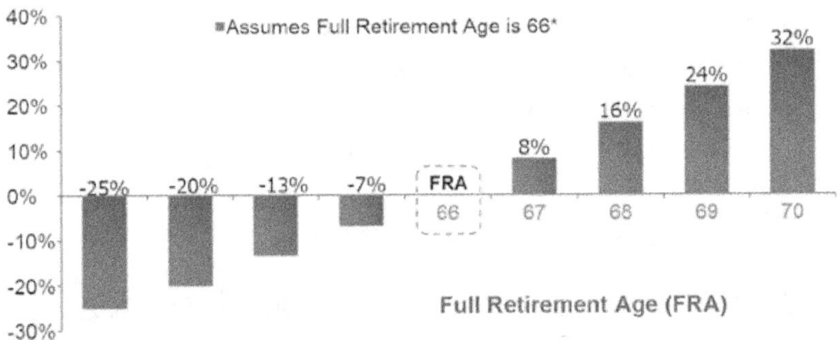

Source: Premier NSSA (www.premiernssa.com)

Monthly Benefit Amounts Differ Based on the Age You Decide to Start Receiving Benefits

This example assumes a benefit of $1,000 at a full retirement age of 66 and 6 months

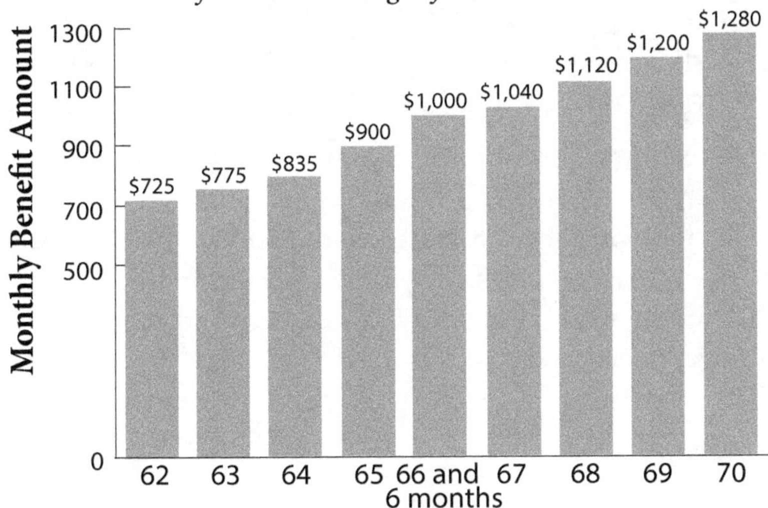

Source: Social Security PDF: "When to Start Receiving Retirement Benefits"

You can see that by waiting or delaying your benefit, you can be paid significantly more. Waiting until 70 sounds like a good idea, right? Yes and no. It depends on your financial situation and the other things to consider, such as expected longevity and health concerns and your desire to leave a survivor benefit (more on this coming up). Far too often, financial institutions and advisors use marketing tactics that mention things like, "We helped John and Jane increase their Social Security lifetime benefits by $250,000!" (sometimes you will see even larger dollar amounts). They do this by illustrating filing at age 70.

Fun Facts

Eligible benefits are based on individual and/or spousal earning records.

Virtually anybody can increase their potential lifetime benefit by waiting until age 70 to file and assuming a life expectancy of age 100. Higher paid benefits for a longer period equals more money paid overall, hence the marketing reference of $250,000 of additional Social Security money.

The following Social Security chart, also found on their website (www.ssa.gov), breaks down the increases and decreases for full retirement ages. It takes a few minutes of studying but lays out the numbers nicely.

Social Security Online

www.socialsecurity.gov   Home   FAQs   Contact Us   Search

Office of the Chief Actuary

Effect of Early or Delayed Retirement on Retirement Benefits

Benefit, as a percentage of Primary Insurance Amount (PIA), payable at ages 62-67 and age 70

Year of birth	Normal Retirement Age (NRA)	Credit for each year of delayed retirement after NRA (percent)	Benefit, as a percentage of PIA, beginning at age--						
			62	63	64	65	66	67	70
1924	65	3	80	86 2/3	93 1/3	100	103	106	115
1925-26	65	3 1/2	80	86 2/3	93 1/3	100	103 1/2	107	117 1/2
1927-28	65	4	80	86 2/3	93 1/3	100	104	108	120
1929-30	65	4 1/2	80	86 2/3	93 1/3	100	104 1/2	109	122 1/2
1931-32	65	5	80	86 2/3	93 1/3	100	105	110	125
1933-34	65	5 1/2	80	86 2/3	93 1/3	100	105 1/2	111	127 1/2
1935-36	65	6	80	86 2/3	93 1/3	100	106	112	130
1937	65	6 1/2	80	86 2/3	93 1/3	100	106 1/2	113	132 1/2
1938	65, 2 mo.	6 1/2	79 1/6	85 5/9	92 2/9	98 8/9	105 5/12	111 11/12	131 5/12
1939	65, 4 mo.	7	78 1/3	84 4/9	91 1/9	97 7/9	104 2/3	111 2/3	132 2/3
1940	65, 6 mo.	7	77 1/2	83 1/3	90	96 2/3	103 1/2	110 1/2	131 1/2
1941	65, 8 mo.	7 1/2	76 2/3	82 2/9	88 8/9	95 5/9	102 1/2	110	132 1/2
1942	65, 10 mo.	7 1/2	75 5/6	81 1/9	87 7/9	94 4/9	101 1/4	108 3/4	131 1/4
1943-54	66	8	75	80	86 2/3	93 1/3	100	108	132
1955	66, 2 mo.	8	74 1/6	79 1/6	85 5/9	92 2/9	98 8/9	106 2/3	130 2/3
1956	66, 4 mo.	8	73 1/3	78 1/3	84 4/9	91 1/9	97 7/9	105 1/3	129 1/3
1957	66, 6 mo.	8	72 1/2	77 1/2	83 1/3	90	96 2/3	104	128
1958	66, 8 mo.	8	71 2/3	76 2/3	82 2/9	88 8/9	95 5/9	102 2/3	126 2/3
1959	66, 10 mo.	8	70 5/6	75 5/6	81 1/9	87 7/9	94 4/9	101 1/3	125 1/3
1960 and later	67	8	70	75	80	86 2/3	93 1/3	100	124

Note: Persons born on January 1 of any year should refer to the previous year of birth.

USA.gov

Privacy Policy | Website Policies & Other Important Information | Site Map
Last reviewed or modified Thursday Aug 19, 2010

Need Larger Text?

Chapter 6

Breakeven

Waiting to take your benefit at age 70 is not necessarily a bad or a good strategy. Ultimately, it is up to you to decide. Most people do not maximize their benefits. In fact, about 57% of people choose to file for benefits before their FRA — for various reasons. One of the most important and determining factors is the need for additional income. Many folks need the money (or just want extra income). However, I believe if people fully understood their benefits, many would choose alternate filing dates/strategies, hence this book's purpose.

On the flip side, by taking your benefit at age 62, you can receive eight years of additional payments! Yes, they are reduced, but you are getting a lower payment for an extra eight years. So, what would the math be on that? This is where a breakeven analysis comes into play. It should not be your only determining factor for filing for your benefit, but it can be a good starting point. Ask yourself: "Will I be able to enjoy my money more between ages 62 and 70 or from age 70 and older?" Most people are not backpacking or water skiing in their 80s. The break-even points are typically 12 to 12.5 years, depending on the age you file — which means if you take your benefit at age 66 instead of age 62, it will take you until age 78 to receive the same amount of money overall, versus taking it at age 62. Similarly, if you wait until age 70 to file versus age 66, the breakeven is at age 82 1/2 because you have received payments (reduced) for an extra four years.

The following chart helps to illustrate the break-even points. It assumes an FRA at age 67 with a PIA of $1,000 per month. The math is roughly the same for each FRA, whether age 66, 66 and 3 months, or 67. The shaded areas show the cash flow totals (not adjusted for any cost of living). Social Security determines increases once per year (and they vary), with some years being zero. Let's take a look at what's going on.

<table>
<tr><td colspan="5" align="center">Break-Even Analysis</td></tr>
<tr><th>Year</th><th>Tom's Age</th><th>File at Age 62</th><th>File at FRA</th><th>File at Age 70</th></tr>
<tr><td>2022</td><td>62</td><td>$8,400</td><td></td><td></td></tr>
<tr><td>2023</td><td>63</td><td>$16,800</td><td></td><td></td></tr>
<tr><td>2024</td><td>64</td><td>$25,200</td><td></td><td></td></tr>
<tr><td>2025</td><td>65</td><td>$33,600</td><td></td><td></td></tr>
<tr><td>2026</td><td>66</td><td>$42,000</td><td></td><td></td></tr>
<tr><td>2027</td><td>67</td><td>$50,400</td><td>$12,000</td><td></td></tr>
<tr><td>2028</td><td>68</td><td>58,800</td><td>$24,000</td><td></td></tr>
<tr><td>2029</td><td>69</td><td>$67,200</td><td>$36,000</td><td></td></tr>
<tr><td>2030</td><td>70</td><td>$75,600</td><td>$48,000</td><td>$14,880</td></tr>
<tr><td>2031</td><td>71</td><td>$84,000</td><td>$60,000</td><td>$29,760</td></tr>
<tr><td>2032</td><td>72</td><td>$92,400</td><td>$72,000</td><td>$44,640</td></tr>
<tr><td>2033</td><td>73</td><td>$100,800</td><td>$84,000</td><td>$59,520</td></tr>
<tr><td>2034</td><td>74</td><td>$109,200</td><td>$96,000</td><td>$74,400</td></tr>
<tr><td>2035</td><td>75</td><td>$117,600</td><td>$108,000</td><td>$89,280</td></tr>
<tr><td>2036</td><td>76</td><td>$126,000</td><td>$120,000</td><td>$104,160</td></tr>
<tr><td>2037</td><td>77</td><td>$134,400</td><td>$132,000</td><td>$119,040</td></tr>
<tr><td>2038</td><td>78</td><td>$142,800</td><td>$144,000</td><td>$133,920</td></tr>
<tr><td>2039</td><td>79</td><td>$151,200</td><td>$156,000</td><td>$148,800</td></tr>
<tr><td>2040</td><td>80</td><td>$159,600</td><td>$168,000</td><td>$163,680</td></tr>
<tr><td>2041</td><td>81</td><td>$168,000</td><td>$180,000</td><td>$178,560</td></tr>
<tr><td>2042</td><td>82</td><td>$176,400</td><td>$192,000</td><td>$193,440</td></tr>
<tr><td>2043</td><td>83</td><td>$184,800</td><td>$204,000</td><td>$208,320</td></tr>
<tr><td>2044</td><td>84</td><td>$193,200</td><td>$216,000</td><td>$223,200</td></tr>
<tr><td>2045</td><td>85</td><td>$201,600</td><td>$228,000</td><td>$238,080</td></tr>
<tr><td>2046</td><td>86</td><td>$210,000</td><td>$240,000</td><td>$252,960</td></tr>
</table>

Source: socialsecurityestimator.com

Tom is eligible for a $1,000 per month ($12,000 per year) benefit if he waits until his FRA at 67. However, Tom decides that he would like to retire early, go to Vegas, and travel the world! So, he files at age 62, and since he is filing at the earliest possible age, he will receive a benefit reduction of 30%.

Why so much? As I mentioned earlier, Tom will be alive longer (statistically), so it will cost the SSA more money over time, which is why it reduces his benefit. Instead of receiving his full $12,000 per year, Tom is only going to receive $8,400. Despite the lower payout amount, he'll receive an additional five years of income — versus waiting until age 67!

If Tom had decided to hold off until age 67 (see the "File at FRA Column"), it would have taken him until age 78 to receive the same amount of overall Social Security benefits. At age 78, you can see that overall payments break even.

Now, if he were to wait until age 70, the latest possible benefit would have started at $14,880 per year. Since he would have waited so long to take his benefit, the break-even difference from filing at age 67 versus 70 would be age 82. So, if Tom knew he would live into his mid-90s and had plenty of other retirement cash flow options, waiting until age 70 could be a great idea.

Let's look at some of the pros and cons of filing at various ages:

Filing at Age 62 (Early):

> **Pros:** *Start getting money ASAP, pay bills, pay off debt, build a travel fund, use cash flow to offset missing income from not working full time, et cetera.*

Perhaps one of the most important factors would be to consider the enjoyment of the money. Are you going to be able to enjoy money more between ages 62 and 78 or from age 78 to 82? Most people tend to slow down a bit in their 80s.

This reduction will also affect the survivor benefit. So, when you pass, your lower-earning spouse would need to rely on less in survivor income than if you had waited for a higher benefit.

Earnings limits are something else to consider. If you are still working and earning an income from either wages or a net profit from self-employment, your Social Security benefit can be withheld if your earnings exceed certain thresholds. IRA income, pension income, annuity income, et cetera do not count toward the earnings limit. How dare you try and take some of your hard-earned, tax-paid money early while still working and paying more taxes?! (More on this shortly.)

Filing at 67 (FRA)

If you are still working, there are no earnings limitations placed on your income. And if you pass away, your survivor benefit will be this amount — without reduction.

Filing at age 70 [Latest]

> **Pros:** *You maximized your benefit to its fullest potential! Since you have waited patiently for so long, the SSA will pay the highest amount for the rest of your life.*

Waiting until age 70 also helps with inflation hedging for your retirement income. Your other income sources and assets that generate income may be fixed payments, limited in growth or exposed to high risk. These factors can make it difficult to keep up with the cost of living/inflation. By filing at age 70, you will also provide the maximum survivor benefits, helping to protect the surviving spouse's cash flow.

> **Cons:** *You had to wait till 70, missing out on payments for eight years (versus filing at age 62).*

The other risk here is your longevity. If you waited until 70 and then passed away shortly after, it may not have been the best rate of return for your individual benefit. Still, your surviving spouse would at least benefit from the delayed retirement credits you earned and never collected.

Social Security Increases and Reductions

Increases and reductions are calculated monthly. Depending on your situation, this can make a big difference when you plan to file for your benefit. By waiting just a few months, you can earn quite a bit more in your monthly benefit for the rest of your life.

Here's a breakdown of the calculations:

Reductions and Increases per Month from Your PIA Benefit Amount

(-)0.417% — Filing at age 62 or more than 36 months from your FRA

(-)0.556% — Filing within 36 months of your FRA

(+)0.667% — Filing after your FRA

Once you know your PIA, you can calculate the monthly reductions or increases.

Fun Facts

Example: Your birthday is in March, and you are turning 66 (your FRA). You delay filing until September and earn delayed retirement credits (DRCs) until you file.

Each month you waited, you added 0.667% to your benefit, equaling roughly 4% (0.667% X 6 months = 4.002).

Let's say you receive your first check in October; it will NOT reflect the increase.

The DRCs earned in the calendar year in which you file are added in January of the following year and then applied to your February check.

If you earned DRCs by waiting to file from previous years, they would be applied immediately upon your filing.

Knowing this, you may want to rethink the timing of taking your benefits.

An exception to this rule: If you wait until 70 to begin your benefits, you will receive all of your DRCs at once with no waiting.

Considerations

Filing your benefit at a particular age is a personal choice based on many factors, but the following are some of the most common considerations:

Income

If you need the money and it's available then, well, you should take it. Keep in mind the earnings limits test that we'll be covering in the next chapter.

Spousal Benefit

If you are eligible for a spousal benefit, you need to consider the reductions in your individual benefit and the spousal benefit. If you file for benefits before your FRA and take the spousal benefit, it will be reduced too.

Survivor Benefit

Consider what your spouse will receive if you pass away. You cannot keep both benefits. If married spouses are both receiving Social Security and one passes, you can only keep the higher of the two benefits. This is where other retirement income planning factors come into play to see if there is enough cash flow to support the lost Social Security income. If there's not, then perhaps the higher wage earner should wait to leave a larger survivor benefit. This situation is common when there is an age difference between the spouses. For instance, if the older spouse has a larger benefit and wants to leave a more significant survivor benefit for his or her spouse, it can be advantageous to wait and let those DRCs build up.

Chapter 7

Filing Before Full Retirement Age (While Working)

The Social Security system uses many complex mathematical formulas to compute your benefit payout. One of the factors that is taken into consideration is age.

Age is important because it helps statistically determine how long your benefit will be paid to you, hence reducing the overall money inside the Social Security trust fund. As I mentioned early, the closer to God you get, the more the SSA pays you because there are fewer payments to send you (statistically speaking). By taking your benefit early at age 62, there is a good probability that you could live to be 80 plus years old. That's 18 years of payments!

Taking this into consideration, the SSA has a set of rules if you take your benefit early. These rules affect all benefits (individual, spousal, and survivor) and can cause reduced benefits on all of them.

Earnings Limit:

If you haven't reached your FRA but are receiving Social Security benefits and still working, you can face a penalty on your benefits. The penalties are fewer in the year in which you reach your FRA. Once you are at your FRA, there are no earnings limits or penalties; you can make $1 million a year without any reduction. Just don't forget that there will be taxes applied to your Social Security benefits if you are indeed earning some good income. More on this coming up soon.

Let's assume you want to take your benefits before your FRA while you are still working, say at 62 years old. Social Security will apply the earnings test, which is as follows:

- Earnings limit of $18,240 in 2020 for any year leading up to the year before you reach FRA

The earnings limit tends to increase each year to keep up with wage growth and the cost of living, allowing you to earn more without a penalty. If you are earning more than $18,240, there will be a reduction in your Social Security benefit as follows: $1 in benefits will be withheld for every $2 in earnings above the limit.

Once you reach your FRA year, the earnings limit is more generous. You can earn a significantly larger amount without a reduction ($48,600 in 2020). The penalty is also reduced as follows: **$1 in benefits will be withheld for every $3 in earnings above the limit. Once you reach FRA and beyond, the earnings limit no longer applies.**

What is the point of the earnings limitation? It is designed to discourage people who are still working and contributing to Social Security from filing for benefits. Most folks are still working at 62 and even 65, but if everyone who turned 62 started taking their benefits for extra cash flow, the Social Security trust fund would hit zero real fast!

Fun Facts

The earnings limits are based on earned wages (i.e., a paycheck from your employer or net profit from self-employment). IRA distributions, annuity payments, dividends, interest from investments, or pension income do NOT count toward the earnings limit.

Earnings limits are based on individual earnings records, regardless of whether you file your taxes as married filing jointly, so your spouse's earnings won't count against you if you are the one filing.

Here's a breakdown to help you visualize the earnings limits (assuming an FRA at age 67):

Age 62 and all months leading up to the year in which you reach your FRA

Income: $50,000

Earnings Test: $18,240

Penalty Basis: $31,760 divided by two

Social Security Work Penalty: $15,880

In this case, Social Security would withhold all checks until the work penalty was fulfilled before resuming monthly payments.

The year you reach your FRA.

Income: $50,000 minus the earnings test

Earning Test: $48,600

Penalty Basis: $1,400 divided by three

Social Security Work Penalty: $467

Social Security would withhold the entire month's benefit, even though the penalty amount is only $467 before paying your benefit in month two.

For many who have already filed, this can come as a big surprise. Lots of folks don't know or take into consideration the earnings test ramifications. What you should do if you plan to take Social Security prior to your FRA is let the SSA know your anticipated earnings and let them calculate your payments. If you do not inform them, you will receive an **overpayment letter**! That's right; you will have to pay back the overpayment amount.

So, what do they do with the withheld amount? Well, they won't go to Vegas with it. Once you reach your FRA, your benefit will be recalculated and adjusted appropriately to reflect the benefits withheld during the time you were working.

For instance, you file for your benefits at age 62 (even though your FRA is 67). A year later, you decide to go back to work. While working, you earn more than the earnings limit and do not receive any Social Security benefits. Once you reach your FRA, Social Security will add back the months they withheld as if you had waited to file, hence increasing your monthly benefit amount to reflect the number of months' benefits previously withheld. In short, you do get your money applied back to you. It just might take a number of years to see the net cash flow difference.

What if you want to collect your benefit halfway through the year, but you have already earned well over the earnings amount?

Well, you're in luck! There is a special earnings rule that is generally used in the first year of retirement. If you retire midyear, you may disregard your earnings prior to your retirement date (provided you earn no more than the monthly equivalent of the annual limit for the rest of the year). Each subsequent year, only the annual earnings test will apply.

For example, let's assume you are making $100,000 per year at age 62, and you want to retire in June. By this point, you have already earned $50,000, which is well above the earnings test. However, when you retire from your job, the SSA will look at your monthly earnings, not your annual earnings.

Here's how it works:

- You file for your Social Security benefit and receive your first check (as long as your earned income in the following months within the calendar year is equal to or less than the 2020 monthly earnings test of $1,520 per month).

- As long as you're below that limit, there will be no penalty or months withheld.

In other words, your earnings before June won't count against you. The monthly earnings test stays in place for that calendar year, after which the annual earnings test applies. If you are filing in the year in which you reach FRA, the monthly earnings test (2020) is higher at $4,050 in those months before you reach your FRA. Be sure always to check the earnings limits. If you are reading this book in 2025, it will be different!

Watch out for additional employer payments or net profits from self-employment. Perhaps your company or business pays out a delayed check, such as commissions or bonuses after retirement; this can affect the monthly earnings test and create a penalty basis for you. What generally does NOT count is vacation or sick pay.

Chapter 8

Spousal Benefits

Spousal benefits are intended to add additional Social Security income for people who are married, divorced, or recognized by common-law states.

When Social Security was created in 1935, the average family had one full-time worker and one full-time homemaker. When the time came for retirement, a single Social Security check may not have been enough to keep the family above the poverty line. Considering this, the SSA created the spousal benefit in 1939, allowing the lower- or no-income-earning spouse to benefit from the higher-earning spouse. In today's world, most couples work, so a spousal benefit may not always be there. The rules to qualify for a spousal benefit are as follows: **up to 50% of the higher earners' FRA benefit**.

Example 1:

- Spouse with $3,000 FRA benefit
- Spouse with $0 FRA benefit

The *potential* spousal benefit would be $1,500, bringing the monthly income to $4,500.

Example 2:

- Spouse with $3,000 FRA Benefit
- Spouse with $1,000 FRA Benefit

The *potential* spousal benefit would be $500, bringing the monthly income to $4,500.

Example 3:

- Spouse with $3,000 FRA Benefit
- Spouse with $1,500 FRA Benefit

There is no spousal benefit since the lower earner's benefit is already 50% of the higher earners.

Did you notice I said "*potential*" benefit? This is because the figures above represent the maximum spousal benefit possible. Depending on your earnings records and at what age you take your benefit, you can face reductions. The younger you file, the lower your payment, similar to your own benefit. One key difference is that there are NO DRCs for spousal benefits. Once you reach your FRA, that's it. They will remain the same.

However, your personal benefit will continue to increase. This is where having a filing strategy is important! By filing for your benefit and your spousal benefit at age 62, you could face a 30% reduction on your individual benefit and a 35% reduction on your spousal benefit.

The upcoming charts assume an FRA of age 67. There are two separate charts for a reason: The SSA calculates benefits slightly differently for spouses who have a working history and those that do not. For spouses without a work history (who are not eligible for their own benefit), Social Security will calculate the spousal benefits based on the working spouse's PIA. If both spouses worked and are both eligible for their own individual benefit, then the spousal benefit is calculated slightly differently. *Why would it be simple?*

For Nonworking Spouses With an FRA of 67

Spouses who are looking to file for a spousal benefit are eligible to receive between 32.5% and 50% of their spouse's PIA. Remember, it's UP TO 50% of the higher earners' PIA.

Example:

John has a PIA of $2,500 per month, and his wife Jane has $0 PIA. If she takes the spousal benefit at age 62, she will receive 32.5% of Johns $2,500, or $812.50. For every year Jane waits, she will receive more until she reaches the maximum of 50% of John's PIA — which will happen once she reaches her (not his) FRA.

For Working Spouses With an FRA of 67

The calculations are slightly different as they are based on the eligible spousal benefit. The eligibility range is from 65% to 100% of the spousal benefit. Using the same example of John and Jane, the spousal benefit is based on 50% of $2,500, or $1,250. If Jane has a PIA of $1,000, she is eligible for $250. If Jane decides to take her benefit at the age of 62, she will receive 65% of the $250 or $162.50. Something is better than nothing!

The following is an example of the reduction amounts right from Social Security's website.

 **Benefit Reduction for Early Retirement**

We sometimes call a retired worker the *primary* beneficiary, because it is upon his/her primary insurance amount that all dependent and survivor benefits are based. If the primary begins to receive benefits at his/her normal (or full) retirement age, the primary will receive 100 percent of the primary insurance amount. If the spouse of a primary begins to receive benefits at his/her normal retirement age, the spouse will receive 50 percent of the primary's primary insurance amount.

The table below illustrates the effect of early retirement, for both a retired worker and his/her spouse. For our illustration, we have used a $1,000 primary insurance amount. With this primary insurance amount and both primary and spouse retiring at their respective normal retirement ages, the primary would receive $1,000 per month and his/her spouse would receive $500 per month. The table shows that retirement at age 62 results in substantial reductions in monthly benefits. Please note that relatively few people can begin receiving a benefit at *exact* age 62 because a person must be 62 throughout the first month of retirement. Thus most early retirees begin at age 62 and 1 month.

Primary and spousal benefits at age 62
(benefits based on a $1,000 primary insurance amount)

Year of birth [a]	Normal (or full) retirement age	Number of reduction months [b]	Primary		Spouse	
			Amount	Percent reduction [c]	Amount	Percent reduction [d]
1937 or earlier	65	36	$800	20.00%	$375	25.00%
1938	65 and 2 months	38	791	20.83%	370	25.83%
1939	65 and 4 months	40	783	21.67%	366	26.67%
1940	65 and 6 months	42	775	22.50%	362	27.50%
1941	65 and 8 months	44	766	23.33%	358	28.33%
1942	65 and 10 months	46	758	24.17%	354	29.17%
1943–1954	66	48	750	25.00%	350	30.00%
1955	66 and 2 months	50	741	25.83%	345	30.83%
1956	66 and 4 months	52	733	26.67%	341	31.67%
1957	66 and 6 months	54	725	27.50%	337	32.50%
1958	66 and 8 months	56	716	28.33%	333	33.33%
1959	66 and 10 months	58	708	29.17%	329	34.17%
1960 and later	67	60	700	30.00%	325	35.00%

[a] If you are born on January 1, use the prior year of birth.

[b] Applies only if you are born on the 2nd of the month; otherwise the number of reduction months is one less than the number shown.

[c] Reduction applied to primary insurance amount ($1,000 in this example). The percentage reduction is 5/9 of 1% per month for the first 36 months and 5/12 of 1% for each additional month.

[d] Reduction applied to $500, which is 50% of the primary insurance amount in this example. The percentage reduction is 25/36 of 1% per month for the first 36 months and 5/12 of 1% for each additional month.

Source: **ssa.gov**

Your spousal benefit is a separate benefit from your own, so you must file for your spousal benefit if you are eligible. Of course, there are rules to claiming your spousal benefit.

Chapter 9

Claiming Your Spousal Benefit

First, let's take a look at the length-of-marriage rules. If you are newly married, you will have to wait at least 12 months, unless one of the two exceptions apply:

1. You are eligible for a child-in-care benefit.

2. You were entitled to benefits from another spouse in the month before your current marriage.

For most people, the 12-month rule is standard. After that time, you are eligible to receive a spousal benefit, considering there is one to be given. You can file for your spousal benefit as early as 62 or as late as 70.

Keep in mind; there are no delayed earning credits for spousal benefits — only for your own benefit — so if the spousal benefit is higher than your retirement benefit, it doesn't pay to wait beyond your FRA.

Now that you have an understanding of spousal benefits, when should you file for them? One thing to consider that is often misunderstood is that you will have to file for your own benefit first and then the spousal benefit, something known as deemed filing.

An exception to this rule applies if you were born on or before January 1, 1954, have reached your FRA and have yet to file any benefits. In that situation, you file what is known as a *restricted application*. Filing a restricted application allows you to file on your current spouse's earnings record and receive your spousal benefit while letting your individual benefit earn delayed credits. The catch is that your spouse (who you are filing for the spousal benefit on) must be receiving their retirement or disability benefit — unless it is your ex-spouse. An ex-spouse does not need to be collecting their benefit, but if they are not receiving their benefit, they need to be divorced for at least two years. More on this later.

Spousal benefits and the process for maximizing benefits with married couples can be a bit confusing. Much of the confusion comes from legislative changes within the SSA. The Bipartisan Budget Act of 2015 was one of the largest changes to Social Security in recent history. In the past, you could have filed for your spousal benefit and not touched your own benefit as long as your spouse (husband/wife) filed for their benefit and suspended it, a process known as *file and suspend*. Today, the rules state that for a spousal benefit to be paid, the spouse you are looking to claim off of must be receiving a benefit, something known as *deemed filing*.

Before the Bipartisan Budget Act of 2015 was implemented, there was a small window of opportunity to avoid deemed filing for spousal benefits. Some people knew about these upcoming Social Security changes and suspended their benefits prior to the April 30, 2016 deadline. As with many governmental changes, they were made quickly without much marketing, education, or public awareness.

Today, there are still folks who are eligible to file a restricted application, which means they can postpone filing for their own benefit and claim half of their spouse's benefit (the spouse must be actively receiving their individual Social Security benefit). In order to take advantage of this filing strategy, you must have been born on or before January 1, 1954, and have yet to file for your own Social Security benefit.

For most people looking to receive a spousal benefit, both spouses need to file for their individual benefit before becoming eligible (unless you qualify to file a restricted application). You can see how this can throw a wrench in the works when it comes to selecting your age in which to file. By filing at your FRA in order to receive 100% of the spousal benefit, you forgo your ability to earn DRCs, which permanently reduces your individual benefit for life. Deemed filing does not apply for survivor benefits (more on this coming up shortly).

It can be a tough decision to start your benefits, especially considering that both spouses will most likely have to file. You must account for your age differences, the spousal benefit amounts, and the survivor benefit amount. Even if you are eligible for a restricted application, it may not be the best scenario for you.

Following is an example of a couple looking to file for spousal benefits:

Jeremy has a PIA of $2,200, and Samantha has a PIA of $600. Her benefit is shown as "Own" on the graph on the following page. You can see if she waits until age 66 (her FRA), she will receive the full $600 in benefits. If she files early or waits, her benefit will adjust accordingly. Since Jeremey has a PIA of $2,200, Samantha is eligible for up to 50% (or $1,100) of his benefit. By filing at 66, she is able to receive her individual benefit of $600 and a spousal benefit of $500, bringing her total to $1,100 per month (up to 50% of Jeremy's PIA). What's interesting about this example is that the overall payable benefits remain the same from ages 66 to 70.

If she waits until age 70, Samantha will have missed out on four years of payable benefits or $52,800. Social Security will not back pay this entire amount. The good news is they will pay back up to six months' worth of spousal benefits (not including any months prior to your FRA). In this example, she would have been better off taking her own benefit at age 66 and filing for the spousal benefit. What is not taken into consideration is Jeremy's age and other financial planning factors. Jeremy would have to file for his benefits at Samantha's age of 66 for the couple to take advantage of this situation.

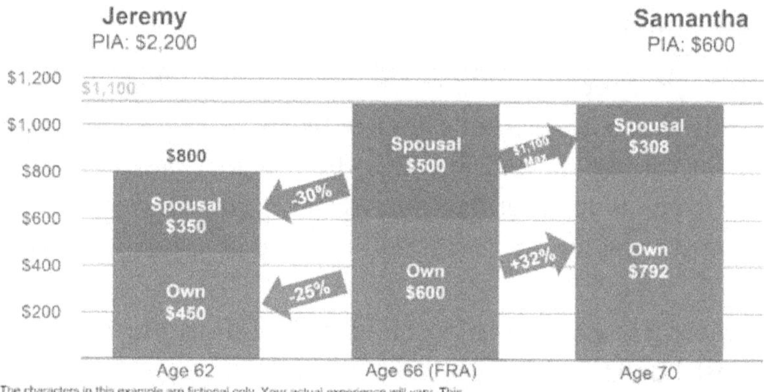

Source: **Premier NSSA**

Another consideration to factor into the spousal benefits formula is the cost of living (COLA) adjustments. The COLAs will add to the increase of spousal benefits. Delaying filing for spousal benefits can increase the overall benefit amount based on COLA adjustments. DRCs will NOT increase the spousal benefit since DRCs only apply to your own retirement benefit.

Here's another example couple:

John's FRA is 67, and he will receive 100% of his PIA ($2,000) at that age. But he waits until 70 to take his benefit, yielding him 24% more ($2,480). His wife, Jane, has a Social Security benefit of $800 per month; the calculation of 50% is based on John's $2,000 per month, not the $2,480.

Now let's assume that the SSA added some COLAs along the way that added up to 5%. His PIA would then be $2,000 + 5% = 100 (and the spousal benefit amount would be calculated on $2,100).

Chapter 10

Divorced Spouses

You can file for spousal benefits on an ex-spouse 1) as long as you were married for at least 10 years, 2) you are currently unmarried, 3) you are at least 62 years old, and 4) your ex-spouse is receiving a retirement or disability benefit from Social Security. If your ex-spouse has not filed for benefits and is at least age 62, you must be divorced for at least two years before making your claim for ex-spousal benefits.

Another strategy to consider: If you were born before or on 1, 1954, you can file a restricted application and claim on your ex-spouse, collecting 50% of their FRA benefit and letting your benefit continue to grow. If you were born after January 1, 1954, you must also file for your benefit (deemed filing). Another rule to keep in mind is that even if you did remarry but later got divorced or your new spouse passed away, then you could file for benefits on your prior spouse(s). Even in the case of multiple marriages, as long as you were married for at least 10 years, you could be eligible on their earning records. You can simply choose the highest paying of them, but you can only receive one of your past ex's benefits — not all of them.

> **Fun Fact**
>
> The earnings limit tests will apply to spousal benefits!
>
> Also, if you decide to suspend your benefit, you will suspend any spousal benefits. Rarely do people suspend a current benefit, but you could. Just know that it will also suspend spousal and child benefits.

Chapter 11

Survivor Benefits

Survivor benefits are payable to eligible spouses as long as the marriage lasted at least nine months. Some exceptions to the nine-month rule are:

- If your spouse dies while in the military

- If your spouse dies as a result of an accident

To start receiving survivor benefits, you must be at least 60 years old unless you are disabled (in that case, you can be eligible at age 50). In cases in which a child at home is under 16 years old or is disabled, a survivor benefit may also be paid.

By electing to take a survivor benefit, you must forgo your benefit and a spousal benefit if you are receiving one. In simple terms, the survivor keeps the higher of the benefits, not both. This is important to consider and a reason you should have some level of guaranteed lifetime income in your portfolio that will cover both lives. The guaranteed, not hypothetical, income source should be enough to cover the difference in the loss of Social Security benefits. This way, your spouse can maintain the same cash flow to support their retirement, lifestyle, and overall well-being.

As mentioned earlier, deemed filing does not apply to survivor benefits. Essentially, you can start receiving survivor benefits at age 60 and let your individual benefit roll up until it is greater than the survivor benefit being paid (as late as age 70). At this point, you can switch to your own benefit.

Keep in mind, the earnings test will apply to survivor benefits, so if you are working and earning an income over those limits, your survivor benefits could be withheld due to your excess income. Depending on your income level, you may not be able to collect survivor benefits at all until you either earn below the limit or you reach your FRA, for which earnings limits do not apply.

Remarrying can also affect your benefit. If you remarry before age 60, you will no longer be eligible for a survivor benefit — unless the new marriage ends by death or divorce. If you wait until after 60 to remarry, you can keep your deceased spouse's survivor benefit.

Note: You are not able to receive a spousal benefit from the new marriage, your own benefit, and a survivor benefit. You have to choose the one that will pay you more — spousal, individual, or survivor.

Again, there are more rules and reductions to survivor benefits. Not only do the earnings limits apply, but the age at which you file for survivor benefits also affects your payout. If you benefit early, it will be reduced just like your own retirement benefit would be reduced if you claimed it early! In fact, two different types of reductions can take place:

1. The age at which the survivor decides to file

2. Age at which the deceased filed or did not file

Let's take a look at the breakdown in the following "Survivor Filing for Benefits" chart for the first option, the age at which the survivor decides to file. You will notice that there are no delayed earning credits for waiting past the survivor's FRA. If the surviving spouse had a potential benefit of $2,000 from their deceased spouse but filed for their survivor benefit early at age 60, they would only receive $1,430 (calculated as 71.5% X $2,000 = $1,430) in this example. In short, the survivor will receive what the deceased was receiving would have been eligible to receive.

 ## Benefit Reduction for Early Retirement

We sometimes call a retired worker the *primary* beneficiary, because it is upon his/her primary insurance amount that all dependent and survivor benefits are based. If the primary begins to receive benefits at his/her normal (or full) retirement age, the primary will receive 100 percent of the primary insurance amount. If the spouse of a primary begins to receive benefits at his/her normal retirement age, the spouse will receive 50 percent of the primary's primary insurance amount.

The table below illustrates the effect of early retirement, for both a retired worker and his/her spouse. For our illustration, we have used a $1,000 primary insurance amount. With this primary insurance amount and both primary and spouse retiring at their respective normal retirement ages, the primary would receive $1,000 per month and his/her spouse would receive $500 per month. The table shows that retirement at age 62 results in substantial reductions in monthly benefits. Please note that relatively few people can begin receiving a benefit at *exact* age 62 because a person must be 62 throughout the first month of retirement. Thus most early retirees begin at age 62 and 1 month.

Primary and spousal benefits at age 62
(benefits based on a $1,000 primary insurance amount)

Year of birth [a]	Normal (or full) retirement age	Number of reduction months [b]	Primary Amount	Primary Percent reduction [c]	Spouse Amount	Spouse Percent reduction [d]
1937 or earlier	65	36	$800	20.00%	$375	25.00%
1938	65 and 2 months	38	791	20.83%	370	25.83%
1939	65 and 4 months	40	783	21.67%	366	26.67%
1940	65 and 6 months	42	775	22.50%	362	27.50%
1941	65 and 8 months	44	766	23.33%	358	28.33%
1942	65 and 10 months	46	758	24.17%	354	29.17%
1943-1954	66	48	750	25.00%	350	30.00%
1955	66 and 2 months	50	741	25.83%	345	30.83%
1956	66 and 4 months	52	733	26.67%	341	31.67%
1957	66 and 6 months	54	725	27.50%	337	32.50%
1958	66 and 8 months	56	716	28.33%	333	33.33%
1959	66 and 10 months	58	708	29.17%	329	34.17%
1960 and later	67	60	700	30.00%	325	35.00%

[a] If you are born on January 1, use the prior year of birth.

[b] Applies only if you are born on the 2nd of the month; otherwise the number of reduction months is one less than the number shown.

[c] Reduction applied to primary insurance amount ($1,000 in this example). The percentage reduction is 5/9 of 1% per month for the first 36 months and 5/12 of 1% for each additional month.

[d] Reduction applied to $500, which is 50% of the primary insurance amount in this example. The percentage reduction is 25/36 of 1% per month for the first 36 months and 5/12 of 1% for each additional month.

Source: SSA (ssa.gov)

Survivor Age	% of Survivor Benefit
50-60	71.50%
61	75.58%
62	79.65%
63	83.72%
64	87.79%
65	91.86%
66	95.93%
67	100%
68	100%
69	100%
70	100%

Assuming FRA is age 67. From ages 50 through age 59 the survivor must be disabled.

Source: **Roy Snarr**

The second option: The potential benefit amount can vary depending on when the deceased filed or delayed filing file for their benefit. For instance, let's assume that the deceased spouse filed for benefits at age 62 or any time before their FRA. In this case, they were receiving a reduced benefit for filing early. Staying with age 62 and an FRA of 67, the deceased spouse received a 30% reduction from their $2,000 FRA benefit (PIA). The monthly payments were $1,400, which is $600 less than the PIA. The survivor will receive a reduced benefit in this case, something known as the 82.5% rule. This means that the survivor benefit will never be less than 82.5% of the PIA. In this example, it is $2,000 (calculated as 82.5% of $2,000 = $1,650) in monthly benefits. If the surviving spouse takes the benefit early, the percentage chart will apply to the $1,650 figure, potentially reducing it even further.

For example:

The survivor takes their survivor benefit at age 60 (71.5% X $1,650 = $1,179.75 in payable benefits). This scenario illustrates why it can be ideal to delay taking your benefit because when you pass away, your spouse may be left with much less.

To expand on this: If we assume the deceased did not take their benefit before they died (and they died before or at their full retirement age), then the survivor would be entitled to the full $2,000 per month or whatever their FRA benefit would have been. The 82.5% rule only applies if the deceased started taking their benefit before their FRA.

Now let's assume that the deceased never filed for their benefit and died at age 69. In this case, we take their FRA benefit ($2,000) and grow it by 8% per year, giving us two years of delayed credits or 16% more:

$2,000 X 16% = $2,320.

If the deceased had lived, their benefit would have been $2,320 (which is now the survivor benefit). Even if the deceased had filed for their benefit at age 69 and died immediately after filing, the survivor benefit would be the same, $2,320. Oh, and by the way, COLA adjustments do apply to survivor benefits too.

Chapter 12

Paying Taxes on Your Social Security

Having a portion of your Social Security benefits become taxable is a big surprise for many people. It is important to understand how your benefits are taxed and what percentage of your benefits are taxed. Taxes take away from your net cash flow. The government will get their portion! If you intend to live on a fixed income, be sure to consider your net income, not gross income. It can be frustrating to think that you have worked your entire life, paying taxes all along the way into the Social Security system, and then once you start to receive your benefit, you have to pay taxes yet again on that income! The SSA has a unique way of calculating your potential tax liability.

The formula is as follows:

Your Adjusted Gross Income before Social Security Benefits + Nontaxable Interest + ½ of your Social Security Benefit + = Provisional Income (other adjustments may apply).

Considering this, you can see how most people will be subject to some level of taxation. The SSA uses a threshold of income based on your tax filing status to determine the amount of your Social Security benefits to be taxed. As much as 85% of your benefits may be taxable! While 15% of your benefit will always remain income tax-free.

	No Taxes on Social Security Benefits
Single	Less than $25,000
Married Filing Jointly	Less than $32,000
	Up to 50% of Social Security Benefits
Single	$25,000-$34,000
Married Filing Jointly	$34,000-$44,000
	Up to 85% of Social Security Benefits
Single	Greater than $34,000
Married Filing Jointly	Greater than $44,000

Source: SSA (ssa.gov)

The first step in calculating what your tax bill may be is to take your Social Security benefit and cut it in half.

For Example:

John has a benefit amount of $24,000 per year, divided by two equals $12,000. That $12,000 is automatically added to the tax formula. Then take any other income sources, including tax-exempt income, such as municipal bonds, and add that number to $12,000 to see which bracket you fall into. If your provisional income is greater than $44,000 (married filing jointly), 85% of your benefit is not taken away in tax; rather, as much as 85% is included in your taxable income above $44,000.

Let's break it down:

John and Jane are married and file jointly. John's yearly Social Security income is $24,000, and Jane's is $16,000 for a total of

$40,000. Half of their Social Security income is $20,000. John and Jane have individual retirement accounts (IRA) income via distributions of $24,000 per year. Both have a pension that brings in a total of $12,000 per year. Additionally, they have a brokerage account that generates $5,000 per year in dividends and interest.

$20,000 (½ of Social Security Benefits)

+

$24,000 (IRA Income)

+

$12,000 (Pension Income)

+

$5,000 (Dividends and Interest)
Total Provisional Income = $61,000

Social Security Taxation

- From $0-$32,000 = No taxes on the benefit
- From $32,000-$44,000 = $12,000 X 50% = $6,000
- From $44,000-$61,000 = $17,000 X 85% = $14,450

Total amount of taxable Social Security benefits = $20,450

Two potential cash flow sources that are NOT counted toward the Social Security tax formula are qualified Roth IRA distributions and loans from cash value life insurance. Converting a portion of your IRA to a Roth could be a good idea for future income planning and before you claim benefits. In the year of conversion, the provisional income calculation would include the converted amount. You may want to consider adding cash-value life insurance to your portfolio, depending on your age and health, but be careful. It can be a great way to diversify, but it has to be done correctly. Unlike a Roth, not everyone is a candidate for life insurance. Always speak with your tax advisor!

Chapter 13

Other Social Security Considerations

Many other situations and circumstances come into play when filing for your Social Security benefit that we did not cover in detail. Everybody's situation is different and filing strategies will vary based on many different circumstances. In the following chapter, I will cover some of the other rules to Social Security at a high level — regarding disability and pension income that was earned while not contributing to Social Security during those working years. My reason to add it toward the end of the book with only a high-level explanation is that the majority of people are not subject to these circumstances.

Chapter 14

Disability

SSDI helps millions of Americans with income when they are not able to work and earn an income themselves. As I mentioned at the beginning of the book, my mother became permanently disabled, which is why I began a career in the financial industry. Her SSDI check was our only source of income for many years. Without it, I don't know how we would have made ends meet. Filing for SSDI can be complicated, which is why there are lawyers who specialize in SSDI.

To qualify, you need to have worked and earned some level of Social Security credits. Typically, you need to have at least 40 credits, and 20 of those credits need to have been earned in the last 10 years of working, ending in the year you became disabled. Younger folks may qualify with fewer credits, depending on their age.

Examples:

- Before age 24: Six credits earned in the three-year period ending when your disability starts.

- Ages 24-31: If you have credit for working half the time between age 21 and the time you become disabled.

- For instance, if you become disabled at age 28, you would need credit for three years of work (12 credits) out of the past six years (between ages 22 and 28).

- After age 31: Following is a chart that references the credits needed.

AGE	CREDITS
31 through 42	20
43	21
44	22
45	23
46	24
47	25
48	26
49	27
50	28
51	29
52	30
53	31
54	32
55	33
56	34
57	35
58	36
59	37
60	38
61	39
62 or older	40

Chapter 15

Windfall Elimination Provision (WEP)

More commonly known as the WEP reduction, this provision applies to individuals who have worked for a government employer that did not withhold Social Security taxes from earnings. This situation is most common with certain state and government jobs and varies by employer, state, and job type. Instead of paying into Social Security, many of the employees will pay into a pension fund provided by the state or federal government that will provide a future benefit similar to what the employee would collect from Social Security. If you've worked or are working for an employer that does not withhold Social Security taxes, your social security benefit will most likely be impacted, creating a reduction in your overall eligible Social Security benefit. This assumes that you had worked for a prior employer and earned Social Security credits. The WEP does not affect spousal and survivor benefits.

Another rule, known as the Government Pension Offset (which we will cover in the next section), can affect spousal and survivor benefits. Notice how I said, "will most likely be impacted"? Not everyone who has worked for employers that did not withhold Social Security taxes has a WEP reduction. To completely avoid the WEP, you must have substantial social security covered earnings for 30 years or more. (There are a few other exceptions as well.)

First, let's look at the maximum reduction you can face. The reduction will be subtracted from your Social Security benefit. It does not matter at what age you file for your benefit — the penalty will apply once you are simultaneously collecting your social security benefit and your government pension!

The maximum WEP reduction is limited to the lesser the applicable dollar amount ($480 in 2020) or50% of your pension. This dollar amount goes up every year. In simple terms, your Social Security benefit will not be reduced by more than half of your pension or $480, whichever is less. If you have a $500 per month pension, your benefit will not be reduced by $480. Rather, it would be reduced by $250 or half.

On the flip side, if your pension is $2,000 per month, your benefit will be reduced by no more than $480, at least in 2020. For instance, if you are entitled to $1,500 per month in benefit but your pension is $2,000 per month, you will receive a Social Security check for $1,500–$480 = $1,020 (which is still more than half of your pension).

Earlier in the book, I mentioned the bend point formula, which is as follows:

PIA formula

For a person who first becomes eligible for benefits in 2020 or who dies in 2020 before becoming eligible for benefits, their PIA will be the sum of:

Bend Points below

> 90% of the first $960 of their AIME
>
> plus
>
> 32% of their AIME over $960 and through $5,785
>
> plus
>
> (c) 15 % of his/her average indexed monthly earnings over $5,785

When Social Security calculates the potential effect of the WEP, they will use the same formula with an exception: Instead of using 90% in the first bend point, they can reduce it to as low as 40%. This 40% increases by 5% increments beginning with 21 years of substantial. The more working years with substantial earnings you have, the lower your penalty. Once you reach 30 years, the WEP no longer applies because the majority of your working years you paid Social Security taxes. Take a look at the following chart. The percentage column represents the percentage Social Security will use in the first section of the bend point formula (a).

Years of substantial earnings	Percentage
30 or more	90 percent
29	85 percent
28	80 percent
27	75 percent
26	70 percent
25	65 percent
24	60 percent
23	55 percent
22	50 percent
21	45 percent
20 or less	40 percent

Source: **SSA**

Here are the maximum dollar reductions by years of substantial earnings per the percentages referenced above for 2019.

	Years of Substantial Earnings										
	<= 20	21	22	23	24	25	26	27	28	29	30
2019	463.0	416.7	370.4	324.1	277.8	231.5	185.2	138.9	92.6	46.3	0.0

Source: **SSA**

There are certain other instances in which the WEP will not apply to you.

WEP Exceptions:

- You're a federal worker first hired after December 31, 1983.

- You're an employee of a non-profit organization who (first hired after December 31, 1983)

- Your only pension is for railroad employment.

- The only work you performed for which you didn't pay Social Security taxes was before 1957; you have 30 or more years of substantial earnings under Social Security.

The 30 years of substantial earnings exception involves a bit of math in order to determine if you indeed have substantial earnings. Below is a chart of earnings needed (at minimum) over the last 30 years, as of 2019. You can find the updated charts and income requirements on Social Security's website (ssa.gov).

For instance, if you are reading this book in 2025, the numbers for substantial earnings for the years 2020-2024 have yet to be posted/updated. Keep in mind that the substantial earnings are only counted for those years in which you worked and paid Social Security taxes — not just your last 30 years as a government or state employee not paying any Social Security taxes.

Year	Substantial earnings	Year	Substantial earnings
1937–1954	$900	1992	$10,350
1955–1958	$1,050	1993	$10,725
1959–1965	$1,200	1994	$11,250
1966–1967	$1,650	1995	$11,325
1968–1971	$1,950	1996	$11,625
1972	$2,250	1997	$12,150
1973	$2,700	1998	$12,675
1974	$3,300	1999	$13,425
1975	$3,525	2000	$14,175
1976	$3,825	2001	$14,925
1977	$4,125	2002	$15,750
1978	$4,425	2003	$16,125
1979	$4,725	2004	$16,275
1980	$5,100	2005	$16,725
1981	$5,550	2006	$17,475
1982	$6,075	2007	$18,150
1983	$6,675	2008	$18,975
1984	$7,050	2009–2011	$19,800
1985	$7,425	2012	$20,475
1986	$7,875	2013	$21,075
1987	$8,175	2014	$21,750
1988	$8,400	2015-2016	$22,050
1989	$8,925	2017	$23,625
1990	$9,525	2018	$23,850
1991	$9,900	2019	$24,675

Source: SSA

It is important to note that if you are going to be hit with the WEP and have not filed for your Social Security benefit, you must contact the SSA to confirm what your WEP-reduced benefit is going to be. The statements you get online do NOT include any WEP reductions; instead, they assume your normal benefit without the WEP factored into the benefit estimates. You must read further into your statement to see the mentioning of WEP. It is always a good idea to call Social Security to get your exact benefit amount. I know this can be frustrating and misleading, but it catches a lot of people by surprise.

Now let's take a look at the Government Pension Offset. This provision goes hand in hand with the WEP, and it can have drastic effects on your retirement plan if you don't understand how it works.

Chapter 16

Government Pension Offset (GPO)

As mentioned earlier, two factors will affect your Social Security benefits when you have a career that does not withhold Social Security taxes from your paycheck. The WEP penalty affects your individual Social Security benefit being paid directly to you. The GPO affects the spousal benefit and the survivor benefit to which you may be entitled.

For spousal and widow/widowers' benefits, the reduction is equal to two-thirds of the monthly pension being received (when the pension money was earned through an employer, such as a government agency, that did not withhold Social Security taxes).

Spousal Benefit Example:

Let's assume that you are eligible to receive a spousal benefit of $500 per month. You also have a government pension based on earnings that were not subject to Social Security tax in the amount of $600 per month. Social Security will multiply the $600 by two-thirds, which equals $400. Then they will subtract that $400 from your spousal benefit, leaving you with $100 in spousal benefits, not the original $500.

Example 2: (using a different set of numbers):

John's pension: $3,000
John's Spousal Benefit: $1,500
Net spousal benefit: $0
Two-thirds of $3,000 = $2,000

John would normally be entitled to the higher of his own retirement benefit or the spousal benefit.

Suppose John's wife, Jane, has a Social Security benefit amount of $3,000. John's Social Security benefit is zero since he spent his entire career in noncovered government employment. Under the GPO in Example 2, he would be entitled to the lesser of a maximum of $1,500 spousal benefit or the actual spousal benefit — up to 50% of Jane's — which is $1,500. Once the GPO is factored in, it would be zero (since two-thirds of $3,000 is $2,000, which is greater than $1,500).

Like the WEP, the GPO only comes into play when you are receiving both benefits at the same time. If it makes sense, you can simply take the Social Security benefit first and later take your pension (or vice versa).

Keep in mind that spousal benefits do not earn delayed earning credits. Once you reach your FRA, that's it; they will no longer increase. You can see how there is a delicate balance. By waiting until after your FRA, your individual benefit will grow, netting you more. However, your spousal benefit will not. Remember, the GPO and WEP only affect the individual with a pension earned by not paying Social Security taxes. Depending on the spousal benefit amount, along with the two-thirds calculation, your spousal benefit and survivor benefit can equal zero.

Survivor Benefit Example:

Using John from the previous example, let's say that Jane passes away. Under normal, non-GPO circumstances, John would be entitled to Jane's $3,000 survivor benefit in addition to his government pension.

In this situation, the GPO two-thirds rule will take effect since John is receiving a pension from his past employer in which he did not have any Social Security tax withholdings. Social Security will look at Jane's $3,000 and apply the GPO rule of two-thirds to it (or $2,000), leaving John with $1,000 in survivor benefits. This will create a significant drop in overall income for John, which is why it is important to have additional guaranteed income streams inside of your retirement plan to help fill the voids.

Are the WEP and GPO fair? The words fair and government are not usually found in the same sentence. The WEP and GPO rules were put into place to protect the overall solvency of the Social Security fund and to eliminate nonearned benefits being paid. Since John did not pay into the Social Security system, why should he have the same benefits payable to him as someone who did? This is why the GPO and WEP were put into place.

Chapter 17

Determining When to Take Your Benefit

"Roy, when should I take my benefits?"

This is by far the most common question I get asked when it comes to Social Security income planning. Ultimately it is 100% up to you! I know this is not the answer you are looking for, but everyone is different. The best way to determine when you should take your benefit is to know your numbers. Read through this book a few times to understand how your benefit is calculated. Understand the dollar amounts at different ages. I suggest taking the following steps:

1. Create an online account with Social Security and download and review your statement.

2. Read through your benefits carefully and make sure everything looks correct.

3. Start calculating the reductions and increases to your benefit and your spousal benefit.

4. You can call Social Security or go into one of their offices and provide them with various filing dates to determine what amount you would be eligible for based on different ages. (A variety of online calculations are also available at www.ssa.gov.)

5. If you plan on taking your benefit early, be sure to review the earnings limits for the year that you plan on taking your benefit.

6. Be mindful of the survivor benefit. What will be left if you or your spouse passes?

7. Be sure to check for any survivor or spousal benefits on an ex-spouse.

8. Calculate any applicable effects of the WEP or GPO.

9. If you were born before or on January 1, 1954, have reached your FRA, and have not already filed, be sure to inquire about a restricted application and the payout amounts.

10. Speak with your financial planner, advisor, and CPA to determine your other income strategies and taxes.

Social Security will answer your questions, but they will not provide any advice on filing. Hopefully, this book has provided enough detail for you to ask the right questions and get the answers you need.

Chapter 18

Other Considerations

I work with folks from coast to coast, helping them maximize their Social Security benefits and creating a retirement income plan they can never outlive. When it comes to retirement happiness, the key to success is income (guaranteed income).

Most advisors specialize in the accumulation of assets, helping you pick the best strategy to grow your money, which is a much-needed service and is important during your working/contributing years.

However, not too many advisors or agents specialize in the distribution of your accumulated assets. Having your assets last while safeguarding against inflation and long-term care costs is essential. Earning interest is important, but having your interest and principal pay you directly into your pocket is more important. It's all about the cash flow and what you can spend to enjoy your retirement — visiting with your kids and grandkids, traveling, or whatever else you want to do. After all, you have worked your entire life to have a retirement. You should spend your time the way you want, eliminating as many worries as possible.

Statistics prove that people live longer and have a better quality of life when they have multiple retirement income streams. At a minimum, you should have a cash reserve equal to six months of living expenses or a minimum of $50,000 that is 100% liquid! Yes, you will not receive much if any interest, but at least you have access to it in case of an emergency. Without it, you will be forced to whip out the high-interest-rate credit card or pull from your retirement accounts in the event of an emergency or if your kids or grandkids need a loan. You need to create a retirement budget!

In addition to your emergency funds, have a detailed budget laid out. Take a look at all your fixed expenses first: your mortgage, property tax, average utility bills, car payments, health insurance, life insurance, long-term care insurance, grocery bills, TV and internet expenses, and loan repayments (credit card, student loans on kids and any other type of financing you have).

Ideally, you should work toward paying down and off all revolving credit debt, starting with the highest interest rate cards first. After you have determined your fixed expenses, look at your discretionary expenses: going out to dinner, vacations, concerts, and shows. Once you have these numbers, add them up and compare them against your guaranteed income streams.

For instance, let's say that John and Jane have a fixed expense of $2,500 per month. Their combined Social Security and pension payments equal $2,000. There is a $500 per month shortfall that needs to be replaced with guaranteed income at a minimum. Their discretionary income budget is $1,000 per month, bringing their total budget to $3,500. Now they should have at least $1,500 per month in guaranteed income.

Why is guaranteed income so important? Because you can count on it. Simply having money involved in the market is hypothetical income (or better put as "if-come" based on average returns and subject to market corrections/losses). Additionally, you are exposed to more than just market risk. You are also exposed to longevity risks, inflation risks, and health risks. If John and Jane have the resources, they can have income provided on a guaranteed basis covering the shortfall of $1,500 per month that can keep up with inflation, allowing them to enjoy retirement and not worry about global conflicts and stress out about the markets. No one wants to fret over the morning and evening news, wondering if they will have enough money to last them.

There are ways in the financial industry to create guaranteed income while maintaining the ability to receive interest, access your funds, create leverage for any possible long-term care situation, and pass along the money to your heirs — without being subject to market crashes. I'll be releasing a separate book about this topic.

Ask yourself the following questions:

- Am I willing to lose a large portion of my money in the market and wait seven to 10 years just to break even?

- Am I willing to go back to work if I lose money because I won't have enough in retirement?

- Am I concerned about the rising cost of healthcare and how I will pay for it?

- Am I willing to spend/liquidate/pay taxes on my entire life's effort of accumulating assets just to pay for long-term care?

- Am I confident that my money will last me and keep up with inflation where it is now?

- Am I willing to have a second, third, or fourth opinion (or more) regarding my retirement income strategy?

- Am I worried about my surviving spouse after I pass away and if they will have enough money to live comfortably?

Chapter 19

Separate Your Specialist

Be sure to have a specialist in your retirement corner, not a generalist!

You should have:

- A risk-money person who helps you with stock picks, mutual funds, bonds, et cetera

- An estate planning attorney who helps you design your will/trust

- A CPA who helps you maximize your tax strategies

- A safe-money person who helps you with income planning and protection of your assets

My passion is helping people with safe money strategies. I am the person who helps folks provide reliability and consistency with a portion of their retirement. It is an amazing and rewarding feeling. Knowing that I help protect retirement assets with income planning, long-term care planning, and legacy planning gets me up in the morning and keeps me going throughout the day. I absolutely love what I do and have been fortunate enough to have made lifelong friends with my clients and continue to build relationships day after day.

If you would like to connect with me, please feel free to do so. You can sign up on our email list for important industry updates or as a means to contact me.

Contact Roy:

Website: roysnarr.com
Email: info@snarrinsurnce.com
Phone: 512-763-2755

About the Author

When I was 14 years old, my mother became permanently disabled. She was sideswiped by a driver who ran a stop sign. The accident accelerated her degenerative disc disease. Shortly after, she was unable to work, and we lost our home and had to move four hours away to my grandparents' house. These events happened during the dot-com bubble, and my mother lost most of her savings and retirement assets in the stock market crash. The only source of income we had to rely upon was her Social Security disability income check. It was not much, but it did help us out dramatically.

Shortly after these trying times, I watched three grandparents live through long-term care situations. Not only was it financially draining on our family, but it was also incredibly emotional. None of my grandparents had any long-term care insurance, leaving the financial responsibilities to their savings and our family.

My family came from a blue-collar background and had no professional financial experience. During high school and college, I worked on my father's logging farm in Missouri, and during the school year, I worked construction and landscaping in California.

Before establishing my career in the financial industry, I had always wondered how a single life event, such as an auto accident, could completely alter a family's entire financial world.

Over the past decade, I have been fortunate to have my mother work with me, and together we have helped educate thousands of people on how to protect their hard-earned money from life's surprises.

Roy Snarr specializes in asset protection, long-term care, and retirement planning and is the host of Safe Money & Income Radio, broadcasting throughout central Texas. He is sought after nationally and helps people across the country with life insurance, long-term care, and guaranteed retirement income planning.

Roy is a Certified Financial Fiduciary (CFF), a Life and Annuity Certified Professional (LACP), and a National Social Security Advisor (NSSA) certificate holder and is a proud member of Million Dollar Round Table (MDRT), the top 1% of licensed financial professionals in the United States.